Hikaru Noguchi's Darning

repair

make

mend

Hawthorn Press

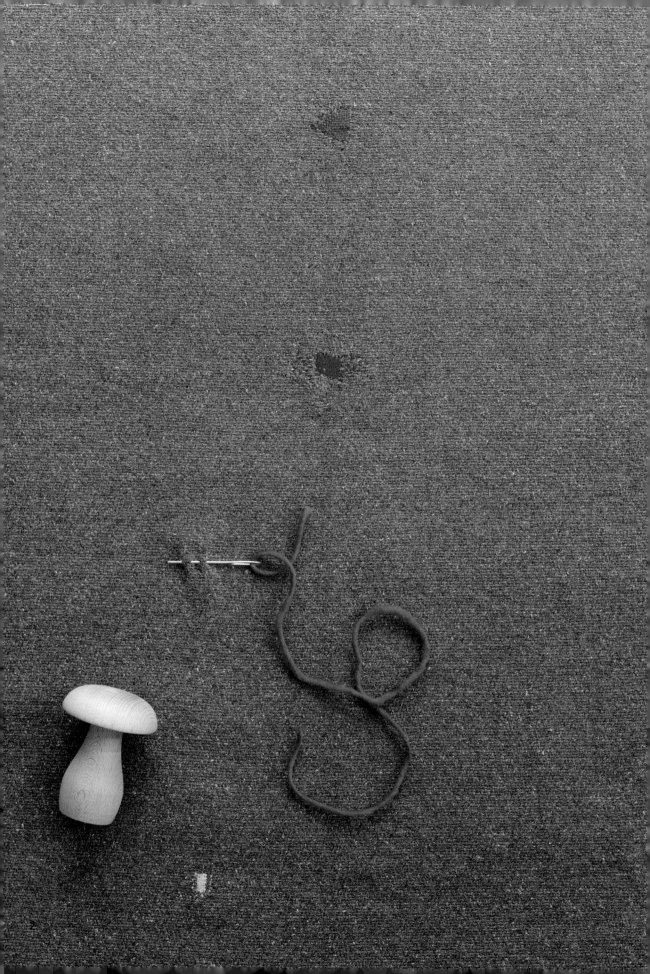

Foreword

When I was little, I was surrounded by old things. My grandfather's hobby was collecting antiques and art. My mother, who taught knitting, used to unravel old sweaters and make skeins. When my father was young, he bought a car that he continued to use for 40 years. I grew up knowing the fun that repairing and continuing to use things could bring. During school, Miss Chandler, a missionary and English conversation teacher from England, wore summer dresses and jackets with black spots where the darned repairs were. I would look at her and think, 'Why don't you buy new clothes?', but I also knew that she was 'chic'. This was my formative experience of darning.

When I first travelled to England at the age of 19, I felt at home with the British way of life where the 'preservation of old things' and at the same time 'new values' were norms of society. I lived in England for another 15 years with this comfortable feeling.

But now times have changed. In the blink of an eye the world has become a place where it is cheaper to replace most things than it is to repair them. As a designer, who for more than 25 years has proposed new designs and products, I have come to question the contradictions of the fashion and design industries. What I found when I first came to England was a form of needlework, darning, in which the mended parts stand out; this suggested a way to solve some of those contradictions.

As time passes, you become attached to things and less keen to keep buying more stuff. So the purpose of darning is not simply the craft. If you think 'Is it okay to mend it myself?' then just go ahead and do it.

My wish is that many more items will be used to the full and when, finally, they can no longer be used they'll return to the soil. Then maybe darning will really become 'part of the world' again.

Hikaru Noguchi

Contents

Contents

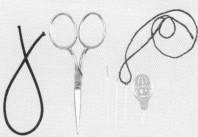

A

B

www.rachaelmatthews.co.uk
Photography: Pictures C, D, E, H
by Kumi Saito; others by Hikaru Noguchi

Darning in England

I had never heard the word 'darning' in Japan. In English it means 'mending,' as they used to do back in the day. It is a simple way of mending at home.

C

A, B: The landscape of Rachael's home in the Lake District. The bridge was designed by her father, an architect. C: A sweater that Rachael has continued to darn. D, E: The yarn that Rachael chooses is colourful. Hers is a method of mending that challenges preconceptions. F: The shop 'Prick Your Finger' that Rachael used to trade in. G: The shop sold craft tools and kits as well as wool. H: Rachael's tools are carried in a pencil case. I: Trunks and branches of trees that fell in a storm, being used by Rachael's father for kindling and woodwork. J: A darning mushroom's head and handle are made separately before being combined. K: Rachael's father working at the lathe.

E

D

F

G

H

Clothes used to be precious. During Queen Victoria's era, most people sewed their own clothes at home and continued to wear and mend them carefully. If you look at the beautifully decorated darning tools and sewing boxes in museums, you can see that mending was an integral part of the culture. During World War II, when there was a shortage of supplies, the government encouraged simple living and recommended darning using a mushroom. You can still find old darning mushrooms in flea markets and sewing boxes from the war generations, stored with small rolls of yarn, like bandages in a medicine chest.

I had my life-changing moment in England when I visited the yarn shop 'Prick Your Finger' run by knitting and textile researcher Rachael Matthews. There I found a darning mushroom and received instructions in its use right then and there. This was when I saw the sweater in the picture. Although the sweater' was mass produced, it was a present and much cherished. After it has suffered repeated washing and many holes, a new mosaic-like stratum was created by darning using colourful wool. I – who used to say, 'Make it look as good as new' and 'I promise mended holes won't be seen' – have realised that this simple method of visible mending can be a means of expression. A shocking experience for me. The darning mushroom made by Rachael's father, an architect and craftsman, was made from thick dried branches broken by the wind from trees in his home in the Lake District. This is the spirit of ingenuity – making the most of the materials you find around you.

Currently in the UK, Rachael Matthews, Celia Pym, Freddie Robbins, Tom of Holland, Amy Twigger Holroyd and Sanae Kido are all active researchers in the art of darning.

I

J

K

The repair studio

For me, darning is an everyday thing – my work is usually on the dining table

When I was living in South Africa, in the morning at the weekends and during long holidays, when the children were studying at the dining table, I started 'dining table crafting' in order to see the children's reaction. On the table were textbooks, notebooks, dictionaries and next to them a sewing box. Soon we started making crochet blankets for the school bazaar and charity events and I would repair the family's clothes by reattaching buttons or altering hems. Hence, my darning workshop is my dining room table. Yarn and tools are put in containers, antique picture plates, silver bowls, baskets and sieves, vintage trays and biscuit tins, anything that looks good. Yarn types are also sorted into easy classifications such as silk-like mohair, wool and metallic lamé. There is also a sweet box for yarn ends that are unclassifiable. It is like a treasure box; it is so much fun to find remnants there. I'm not the type who can tidy up easily, but thanks to

this wonderful storage system I sometimes find an unexpected combination of threads and colours.

The beauty of darning is that most projects are finished within a few minutes to an hour. There's no need to take out a sewing machine; the tools are as simple as a darning mushroom, needle and scissors. You can darn just as quickly as sewing on a button. If you're set on darning a larger area, you can continue to enjoy the pleasures of sewing and working methodically, giving you a great sense of satisfaction in a job well done.

Darning is similar to sewing on a button. Even if it is not done in the 'right way' published in a book, you still somehow manage to do it. Although this book has 12 patterns from basic to advanced techniques, none of these needs to be followed exactly to the letter. It is fine if you just somehow manage to do it. Through repetition, the stitches will start to become your own original creation.

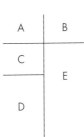

A: A lot of mohair is produced in South Africa, where I lived for a long time. B: I pile up a myriad of colourful wools and place them beside my dining table. The more colours and materials, the greater the creativity. C: An African basket full of darning mushrooms. Even the decorative ones still get used. D: Absorbed in the moment for a few minutes when darning. E: My favourite mushroom and thread in a wicker basket for easy access.

Vintage darning mushrooms

- -

If you visit any museum about daily life in Europe, you can see displays of darning mushrooms and sewing boxes. I still see them frequently in European and American markets and antique shops. There are various types besides the basic darning mushroom. There's a darning shell in the shape of a cowrie, a darning egg, a darning lollipop, a darning foot for the lower part of the shoe, which looks like a shoe mould, and a darning stick used only for gloves. When I see the marks and scratches on one I think of who used it and what they were thinking as they darned.

A: Palm-sized mushroom with a painted rose design. B: Plastic mushroom with a marble pattern which stores needles and thread inside. C: Hand carved wooden mushroom. D: This mushroom has a metal ring to hold the material. E: This one is specifically for socks. F: The cabbage press is a kitchen utensil, but some museums say that it was used for darning too. G: Flower painted. H, D: Mushrooms with metal band. I: Plastic mushroom made in 1950–60. J: A simple mushroom bought in a flea market.

Original darning mushrooms

I wanted to make the ideal darning mushroom, so I worked with Hachioji woodworking factory to make prototypes. Apprentices at the workshop noted the daunting task of holding a darning mushroom in the left hand while sewing with the right and so we invented a standing mushroom that could be placed on a table. The idea is based on a carved figurine from South Africa that I use as a mushroom for darning big holes. We also offer original mushrooms unique to Japan, such as Kokeshi mushroom dolls made by a craftsman in Miyagi and marble mushrooms from Gifu.

A: Made with Nordic beech, this was polished with dark brown oil. B: Shaped like the mushrooms found in picture books about forests. C: Can be placed on the table or held in the hand. As it is lightweight, it is perfect for long periods of darning. D: Made from Gifu marble. Because it is heavy it is useful for darning denim and other heavy material. E: Produced in collaboration with a master craftsman from Miyagi. I had the waist made thinner so the piece is easier to hold and the head made oblong and flat. F: Especially for darning five-toe socks.

Let's start darning

What you need

As long as you have a darning mushroom you can darn with any sewing tools in the house. Once you have to hand an elastic cord, scissors, needle and needle threader you are ready to start.

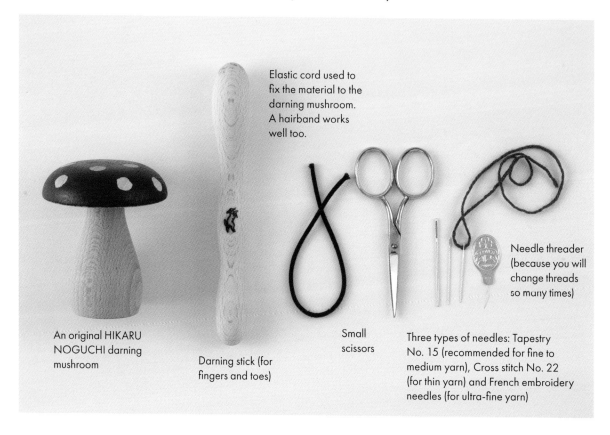

An original HIKARU NOGUCHI darning mushroom

Darning stick (for fingers and toes)

Elastic cord used to fix the material to the darning mushroom. A hairband works well too.

Small scissors

Needle threader (because you will change threads so many times)

Three types of needles: Tapestry No. 15 (recommended for fine to medium yarn), Cross stitch No. 22 (for thin yarn) and French embroidery needles (for ultra-fine yarn)

HIKARU NOGUCHI Darning Mushroom

❶ The mushroom head is painted with cute polka dots

❷ High-quality white wood. It should feel comfortable in your hand and smooth enough to use for a long time

❸ The flat base means you can work with it on the table

Darning stick

Ideal for five-finger socks or gloves, which both tend to wear easily. Use the thicker side for thumbs and the thinner side for fingers.

Darning Technique 1   S e e d   s t i t c h

Seed stitches are so named because they look like scattered sesame seeds on the surface of your work. It is a technique used to reinforce worn-out fabrics such as heels in socks.

<< When to use >>

When there isn't a hole but the fabric is worn or damaged

Before

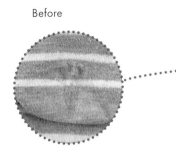

After

Yarn:
Synthetic hair thread (orange)
Sashiko thread (yellow)

Setting up the darning mushroom

1   Place the worn area over the darning mushroom. Stretch the material over and hold it tightly.

2   Wrap the elastic cord round the base of the darning mushroom.

3   Tie the elastic cord once (don't tie it twice in case it won't come undone).

First row

4   Place the worn area over the darning mushroom. Stretch the material over and hold it tightly.

5   Take a stitch from about 5mm (¼in) outside the worn area, starting at the top right corner, 1cm (⅜in) from the right.

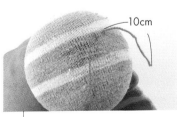

6   Pull the thread and leave about 10cm (4in) at the end to tidy up later.

Lesson 1

7 For the second stitch go back 1–2mm (³⁄₈in–³⁄₄in) from the first stitch and then stitch from right to left.

8 Stitch about 1cm (³⁄₈in) further. A seed stitch will appear on the front.

9 Continue to do one stitch forward and a seed stitch back (see the diagram on p15). Complete the row.

Second row

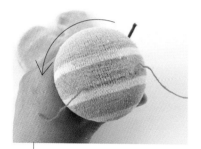

10 After one row, rotate the darning mushroom 180 degrees.

11 Just above the first row, start sewing the second row from right to left.

12 The second row should not be aligned with the first row but sewn randomly.

Change colour

13 When the yarn runs out, change the colour. Remove the thread from the needle and change the thread leaving the end loose.

14 When you start the stitch with the new thread continue with seed stitch as before.

15 When you sew, follow the worn area and a pattern will naturally form.

Tidying the thread

16 | Pull off the elastic cord and remove the material from the darning mushroom.

17 | Tidy the threads from the start of sewing or where the yarn was changed. Thread the end through the needle and push it through to the back of the work.

18 | Turn the fabric over and weave through four stitches.

19 | Splitting the darned threads, weave back through another two stitches. After tidying the thread, lightly apply steam with an iron to set the thread.

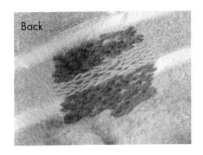

Back

The stitches tightly cross over each other on the reverse, reinforcing the fabric. You normally sew the seed stitch from the front, but if you wish, you can darn it from the back so this side shows.

Seed stitch

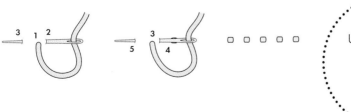

<< Tip! >>
Unlike a normal backstitch, the trick is to go back by just 1mm ($\frac{1}{16}$in)

Darning Technique 2   The square

This is the most basic darning technique that secures the warp and weft threads and you'll even be able to fill wide holes cleanly. Changing the colour of the yarn makes it look even more interesting.

<< When to use >>

From small moth-eaten holes to heavily torn holes

Thread used:
Fine thread in yellow-green and pink

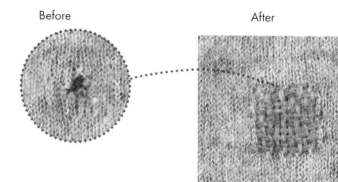

Before

After

Sew the warp

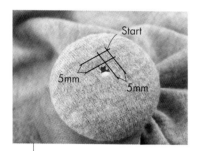

1 | Set up the darning mushroom. Start the first stitch from 5mm (¼in) outside the top right of the hole.

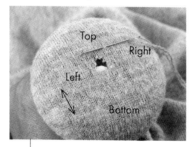

2 | Decide the top, bottom, left and right. Pick up one or two threads of the material. In order to go all the way through make sure the needle hits the mushroom.

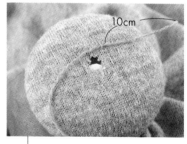

3 | Leave 10cm (4in) of thread at the end to tidy up later.

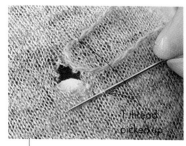

4 | As step 2, insert the needle from right to left, 5mm (¼in) from the lower right of the hole and directly below the first stitch.

5 | When you pull the thread, a vertical line will appear. Pull the thread so that it is neither too loose nor too tight.

6 | Working from right to left, pick up another thread next to the first stitch and one darning thread apart.

Sew the weft

7 Pass the thread from the hole to 5mm (¼in) outside and completely cover the hole. Now the vertical warp is complete.

8 Change to the pink thread to work the weft. First pick up the first thread from right to left at the top corner of the horizontal threads.

9 Pass under the first warp thread but skip the second. Alternate every other thread with the needle. At the end, pick up the left end fabric from right to left.

10 Pull the thread and rotate the darning mushroom 180 degrees.

11 Pick up a thread at the end of the row. The second row should be woven the opposite way to the first row: over the first thread and under the second.

12 At the end of each row, pick up the a thread from the fabric from left to right.

13 Here the second horizontal row has been worked. Continue to weave so that gaps aren't left between the horizontal threads.

14 Rotate again and repeat steps 11 and 12. It may be easier to use the end of the needle so as not to split the thread.

15 Don't sew through the threads. If you split them, the darn won't fill properly. After sewing, apply gentle steam to set the threads.

Thread-tidying variations

Pass through the front of the stitches

This is the easiest method, suitable for clothes such as socks or underwear where the back will be worn next to the body.

1 | While still on the darning mushroom, hide the thread along the inside of the warp.

2 | Then, hide it along the weft, making an L shape.

3 | Cut the thread ends as short as possible.

Pass through the back stitches

This will create a slightly lumpy surface, but it's still okay for clothes that touch the skin.

1 | While still on the darning mushroom, hide the thread along the inside of the warp.

2 | Weave the end of the thread around four stitches at the back.

3 | As in step 2, weave back through another two stitches, then back again through another two, this time sewing through the actual thread.

French knot at the back

Good for small items such as bags and cardigans that do not touch the skin directly.

1 | Remove the material from the darning mushroom and pull the thread through to the back.

2 | Weave the end of the thread around four stitches at the back.

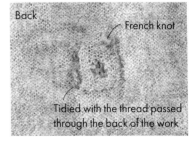

Back

French knot

Tidied with the thread passed through the back of the work

The back is clean with few stitches and the hole is closed with vertical and horizontal threads.

Darning Technique 3 Reversible darn

This technique is almost the same as the square stitch. For anything that is noticeable, such as collars, cuffs, shawls and scarfs, stitch on both sides and make it reversible.

<< When to use >>

Collars, cuffs, scarves, and shawls

Before

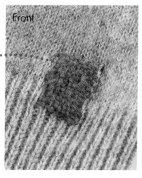

After

Front

Back

Thread used:
Extra-fine woollen yarn
(purple and pink)

Front

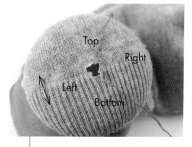

Top
Right
Left
Bottom

1 | Place the front of the material on the darning mushroom and sew a warp thread according to steps 1–7 on p16.

2 | Complete the square darning through the weft by referring to steps 8–15 on p17. Do not tie the ends at this time.

Back

3 | Turn the material over and set the back of the sewn square in the centre of the darning mushroom.

Thread tidying

4 | Sew a second square darn matching the one on the front.

5 | Remove the material from the darning mushroom and insert the thread between the front and back squares.

6 | Pull the end of the thread gently and trim close to the surface.

Darning Technique 4 Seed and square

<< When to use >>

When there's a hole
and the material
around it is worn

This technique combines the basic square and the seed stitch so it is possible to repair the hole and reinforce the material. Change colour every few rows to create a plaid design.

Before

After

Threads used:
Sashiko thread in navy blue, brown and red

Sewing the warp

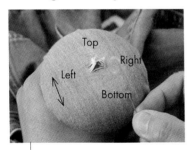

Top
Right
Left
Bottom

1 | Place the material on the darning mushroom. Start with a seed stitch on the lower right of the worn area.

10cm

2 | First take a stitch and pull the thread. Leave 10cm (4in) tail at the end.

3 | Sew one seed stitch, go back 1–2mm (³⁄₈in–³⁄₄in), see p15.

Changing the thread colour

4 | Sew one seed stitch row.

5 | From the first row, take a stitch to the left and do a second row of seed stitch.

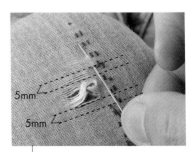

5mm

5mm

6 | On the third row stop the seed stitch 5mm (¼in) before the hole. Skip over and start sewing 5mm (¼in) on the other side.

7 | Pull the thread and continue to seed stitch. Repeat this until the hole is covered.

8 | When the thread runs out change colour. If you change every three or four rows, you'll create a plaid pattern.

9 | Now the hole is completely hidden by the vertical threads.

Sewing the weft

10 | Continue the seed stitch vertically and reinforce the worn parts.

11 | The horizontal thread starts from the upper right, slightly away from the square to reinforce the fabric.

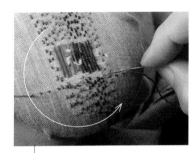

12 | Once the left edge is sewn, rotate the darning mushroom 180 degrees and sew the second row.

13 | When it comes to the square part, weave through the vertical threads and sew seed stitches to the left.

14 | Once the horizontal weave is finished it will create a tartan cross.

15 | Continue the seed stitch several times to reinforce the worn area. Finally tidy the thread (see p15) and steam lightly.

Darning Technique 5   Triangular darns

This is an applied square darn. From changing the way you sew the vertical thread the shape can freely change into triangles or hearts. Drawing the shape first makes it foolproof.

<<When to use>>

Change damage, holes and stains into a pretty needlepoint design

Before

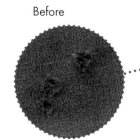

After

Threads used:
Triangle: Weft thread and warp thread, mixed fine yarn (orange)
L shape: Warp, medium fine yarn (khaki); weft, extra-fine mohair yarn (khaki)

Triangle

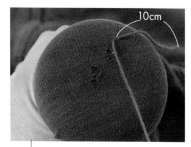

10cm

1 | Pull a small part of the thread from right to left on the upper right side.

2 | Just below the first stitch, make a stitch from right to left in the same way as step 1.

3 | Sew the second vertical line by making a stitch from right to left at a position slightly lower than the first.

4 | The second line will be shorter than the first line.

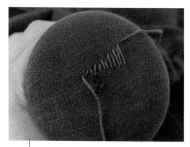

5 | Stitch at a lower position each time to shorten the vertical threads and form a triangle.

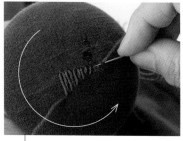

6 | Rotate 180 degrees and pass through the vertical thread. First take a stitch from right to left to make the tip of the triangle.

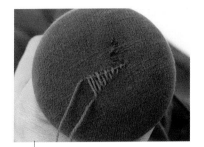

7 | Weave the horizontal thread through the vertical thread (see p17). Take one stitch from the left edge of the material going from right to left.

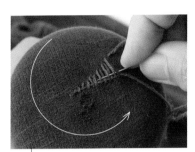

8 | Rotate the darning mushroom 180 degrees and pass the second horizontal line through as you did in steps 6–7.

9 | Here the horizontal weave is finished. When you have tidied the thread (see p18) the triangle is complete.

L-shape

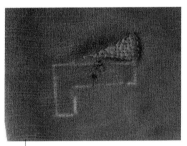

1 | Over the hole, mark the outline of the L with pen or chalk that can be washed out.

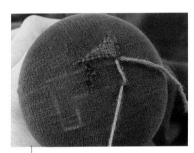

2 | Set the material on the darning mushroom and make one stitch from right to left in the upper right and one just below it, following the chalk line.

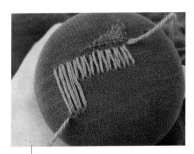

3 | Pass the vertical thread along the drawn outline (see steps 1–7 on p16).

4 | Change to mohair. Stitch from right to left on the upper right. Pick up the left edge of the fabric as you weave.

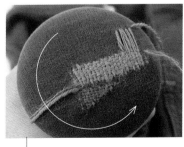

5 | Rotate the darning mushroom 180 degrees while repeating step 4. Fill the long side of the L.

6 | Continue, filling the short side to the end. Finally, tidy the thread (see p18). After sewing, apply gentle steam to set the threads.

Darning Technique 6   English darning

An applied square darn technique used for worn or damaged materials. Picking up a little of the original fabric as you weave means the darned part blends in, giving it a natural finish.

<< When to use >>

When you want to repair the fabric casually and naturally

Thread used:
Weft thread, warp thread
Extra fine woollen yarn (orange, reddish brown)
No. 25 embroidery thread (US floss) (ochre)
Synthetic mix yarn (green)

Before

After

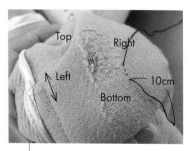

1 | Place the material on the darning mushroom and begin a running stitch about 1cm (3/8 in) below the damaged area.

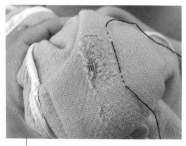

2 | Skip over the damaged part and continue with running stitch up to the top.

3 | Repeat steps 1–2 to complete the warp thread while changing the colour.

4 | Sew the weft. Start from the upper right and do a running stitch as you did on the warp.

5 | Pick up some of the fabric randomly as you weave through the vertical threads. It won't be so neat, but will be more secure and natural looking.

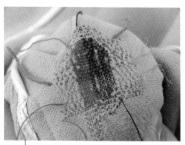

6 | Continue the line with a running stitch until the end and tidy the thread (see p18). Apply gentle steam to set the threads.

Darning Technique 7   Accordion darns

Accordion-style darns use thick thread, such as Japanese paper or ribbon yarn. The weft is a simple seed stitch. You can use thick yarn for the vertical stitch instead of ribbon.

<< When to use >>

Light damage such as slightly worn cloth or stains

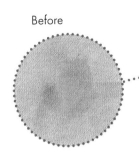

Before

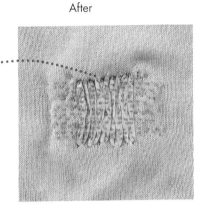

After

Thread used:
Warp, Japanese paper yarn (grey)
Weft, silk hand-sewing thread (khaki)

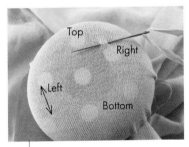

1 Using a quilter's binding needle with a large eye and paper yarn, pick up from the top right of the stain from right to left.

2 Take a stitch from right to left directly below the first stitch and pull to get a vertical thread.

3 Continue the warp in the same way as steps 1–2. Hide the stain with the vertical threads, continuing 5mm (¼in) beyond the edge of the stain.

4 Sew the weft with seed stitch (see p13). First sew from about 1cm (³⁄₈in) in front of the vertical thread on the upper right side.

5 Continue with seed stitch to hold down the Japanese paper thread.

6 Sew the seed stitch for longer on the left if you like. Finally, tidy the thread (see p15) and apply gentle steam to set the threads.

Darning Technique 8   Appliqué

A large hole covered with fabric and scattered with seed stitches
will have more charm than commercially available patches.

<< When to use >>

**To repair large holes
or fabric damage**

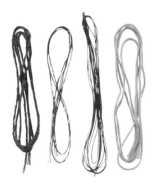

Threads used:
Sashiko thread in green
blue, ochre and red

Before

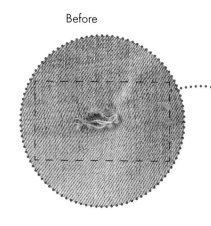

After

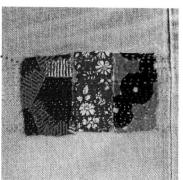

1 | Place a printed cloth that is cut to the size of the hole onto the double-sided interface to make an appliqué (here three patches are used).

2 | Place a cloth over the printed material and interfacing and iron to bind them together.

3 | Remove the release paper from the interfacing, place the patch on the holed part of the jeans and iron.

4 | If you have a large area to sew you can use a bowl with a rounded base instead of a darning mushroom.

5 | First, sew the lower side of the cloth with seed stitch (see p13) from end to end.

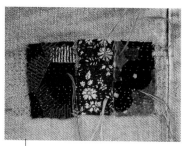

6 | Seed stitch one row at a time from left to right, sewing for 1–2mm ($^3/_8$in–$^3/_4$in), longer on the left. Tidy the threads (see p15).

Darning Technique 9 Reverse appliqué

The cloth is applied from underneath the hole. The hole is stitched around the edges so that it is reinforced and won't tear any further – perfect for denim knees and T-shirts.

<< When to use >>

Use on any item with a medium-sized hole

Before

After

   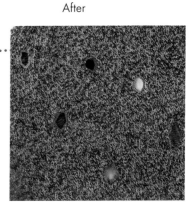

Thread used:
Silk hand-sewing yarn
Wide velvet ribbon
(use any odds and ends you have at home)

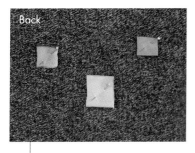

1 | Turn the material over, place the ribbon over the holes and hold them in place with a pin.

2 | Tack around the ribbon and remove the pins.

3 | Turn over the material and set it on the darning mushroom. Work a blanket or buttonhole stitch around the edge (see p49).

4 | Pick up the ribbon with the needle and sew using small, short stitches.

5 | After you have gone around once, secure by working into the first stitch.

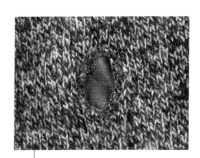

6 | On the back, tidy the thread (see p18).

Chapter 1 | Darning in autumn and winter

Heavy items such as coats and scarves are used for many years and damage can occur. Refresh the look with decorative darning techniques.

01

repair make mend
02

Damage:
coffee stains and a tear
Thread used: mohair
blended yarn
How to make
Sew a honeycomb darn around
the damaged part (see p48).

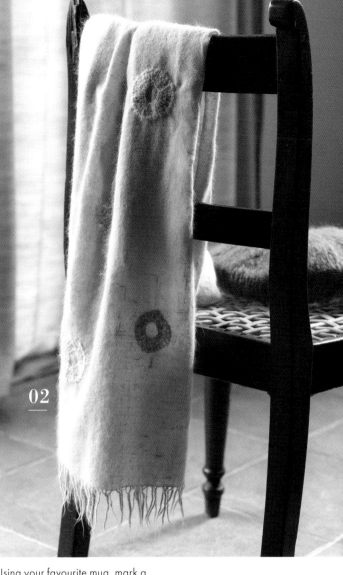

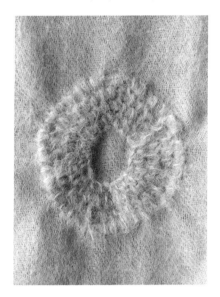

02

Using your favourite mug, mark a
circle around the stains or tears and
sew so that they are hidden. If you
leave the middle unsewn it looks more
like a deliberate pattern.

I chose six bright colours, applied
a small square darn and changed
the moth devoré into an accent.

repair make mend
01

Damage: moth-eaten
Thread used: extra-fine woollen
yarn
How to make
Darn over the hole with a basic
square darn (see p16) on both
sides to make a reversible darn
(see p19)

Chapter 1

repair make mend
03

Damage: wear due to rubbing
Thread used: medium-fine
woollen yarn
How to make
Sew a square darn over the tips
of the index finger and thumb
(see p16).

repair make mend
04

Damage: holes and tears due
to finger friction
Use yarn: extra-fine yarn,
embroidery yarn
How to make
Create a shape to fit the hole
(see p22). A darning stick is
helpful for working the fingers.

Damage: the fingertips are worn
out and a second hole is on the
way. First I embroidered with
the embroidery thread I had
to hand, then darned the part
that was thinned with extra-fine
woollen thread.

03

repair make mend
05

Damage: torn material
Thread used: extra-fine woollen yarn, No. 25 embroidery thread, synthetic mix yarn
How to make
English darn (see p24).

This yellow duffle coat, from established British company Gloverall, sustained some damage. Picking up some of the background fabric helped to blend in the threads naturally.

repair make mend
06

Damage: deterioration
of fabric over time
Thread used: space-dyed
mohair wool
How to make
Darn with seed stitch (see p13)
and square darn (see p16)
and blanket stitch on the worn
edges.

I chose a silk-blended mohair yarn dyed
to a similar colour to blend in with this
classic camel coat. Mohair yarn, with its
elegant lustre and fibre strength, is ideal
for friction damage.

Chapter 2 | Darning socks

Socks are prone to damage: the fabric wears out and there's always holes around the toes. Use durable mohair for your darns to keep them in use.

repair make mend
07

Damage: holes from friction and tearing caused by farm working. Thread used: regular thick yarn
How to make
Darn the hole and the surrounding area with seed and square darns (see p20). Accent the toes of the foot with a varied square darn (see p22).

repair make mend
08

Damage: ageing
Thread used: extra-fine mohair
How to make
Seed stitch the lightly worn
parts (see p13) and chain
darn the worn portion of the
heel (see p49).

repair make mend
09

Damage: ageing
Thread used: extra-fine mohair
How to make
Honeycomb darn to fit the
shape of the heel and the toe
(see p48)

Even if you treat woollen
tights with care they will still
wear down. Honeycomb and
chain darning are the most
effective for this kind of wear.
With these simple stitches
you can continue to wear the
tights for a long time.

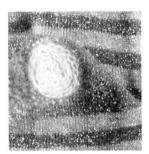

repair make mend
10

Damage: ageing
Thread used: extra-fine mohair yarn
How to make
Honeycomb darn with yellow and
beige mohair (see p48), chain darn
the left heel (see p47)
and accordion darn the right heel
(see p25).

repair make mend
11

Damage: ageing and holes
Thread used: extra-fine woollen
yarn, extra-fine mohair yarn, silk
hand-sewing yarn
How to make
Seed darn in lightly worn areas (see
p13) and square darn in the toe
holes (see p16).

repair make mend
12

Damage: ageing, wear and holes
Thread used: extra-fine mohair
yarn and extra-fine yarn
How to make
Square and seed darn (see p20).
Use English darn for large worn
areas (see p24).

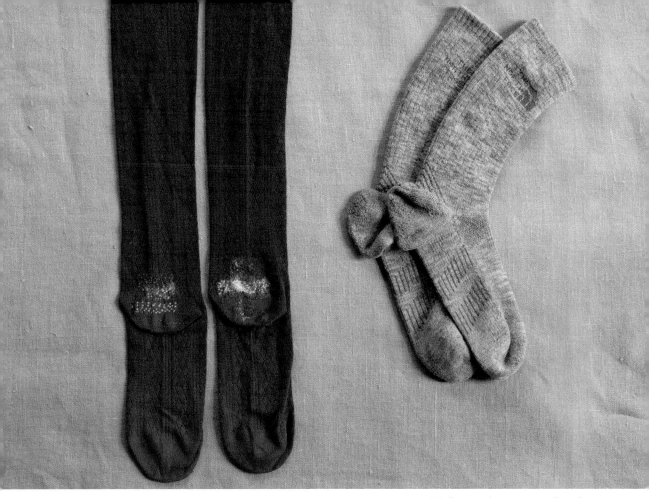

Walking socks in navy and earthy colours are darned with colourful thread to make the stitches stand out.

repair make mend

13

Damage: ageing
Thread used: cotton blend synthetic yarn, extra-fine mohair
How to make
Seed darn the light tear on the left heel (see p13); darn the small hole on the right heel with a seed and square darn (see p20).

repair make mend

14

Damage: ageing
Thread used: cotton blend synthetic yarn
How to make
Honeycomb darn the heel (see p48).

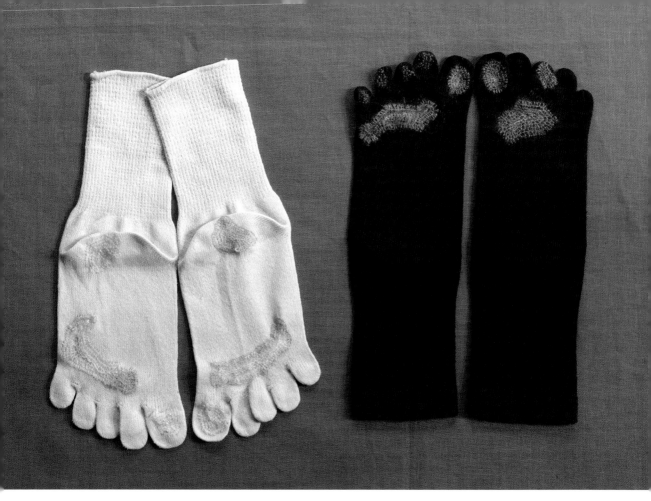

Just like having a pedicure: when the toes have beautiful colours, the feet become vibrant and pleasing. Try choosing a bright colour when you next darn your socks.

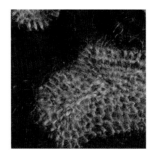

repair make mend
15

Damage: ageing
Thread used: extra-fine
mohair yarn
How to make
Darn the worn parts such as heels
and toes with honeycomb darning
(see p48).

repair make mend
16

Damage: ageing
Thread used: extra-fine
mohair yarn
How to make
Darn the worn areas of the toes
with honeycomb darning (see p48).

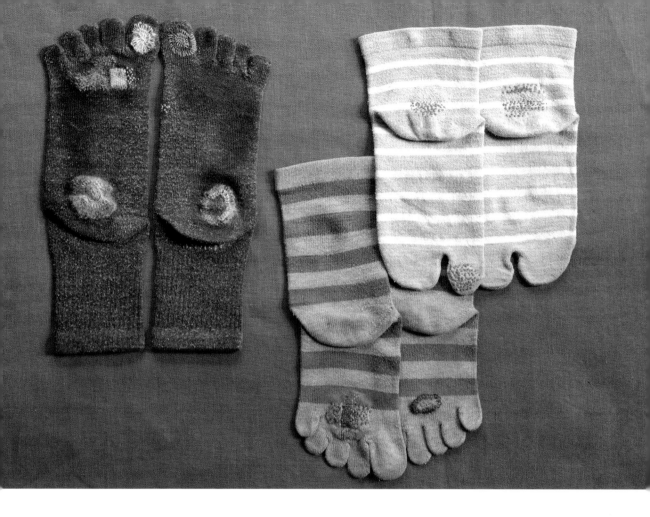

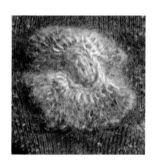

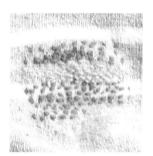

repair make mend
17

Damage: ageing and holes
Thread used: extra-fine mohair
yarn and synthetic yarn
How to make
Darn the worn parts such as heels
and toes with honeycomb darning
(see p48). Darn the hole with a
seed and square darn (see p20).

repair make mend
18

Damage: ageing and holes
Thread used: extra-fine mohair
How to make
Darn the left hole with seed and
square darn (see p20). Darn the
small worn part on the right with
honeycomb darn (see p48).

repair make mend
19

Damage: ageing
Thread used: sashiko thread
How to make
Darn the heel and the worn parts
of the big toe with a seed stitch
darn (see p13).

20

22

23

21

Chapter 3 | Darning denim

Denim is surprisingly easy to darn and will match any thread or design. Appliqué, darn and decorate the holes. Sew this versatile material without over-thinking for spontaneity.

24

25

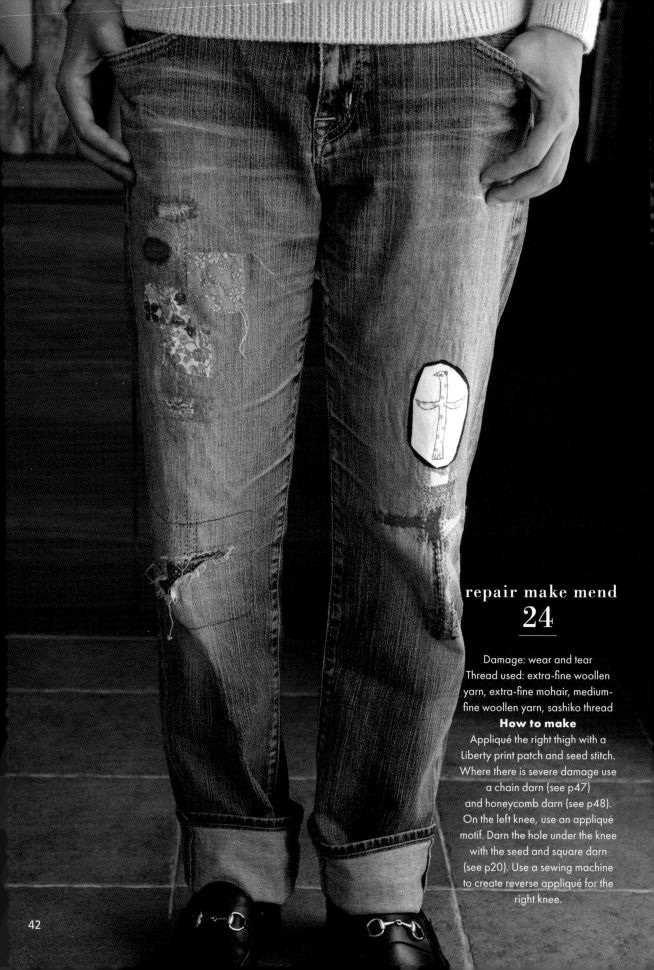

repair make mend
24

Damage: wear and tear
Thread used: extra-fine woollen
yarn, extra-fine mohair, medium-
fine woollen yarn, sashiko thread
How to make
Appliqué the right thigh with a
Liberty print patch and seed stitch.
Where there is severe damage use
a chain darn (see p47)
and honeycomb darn (see p48).
On the left knee, use an appliqué
motif. Darn the hole under the knee
with the seed and square darn
(see p20). Use a sewing machine
to create reverse appliqué for the
right knee.

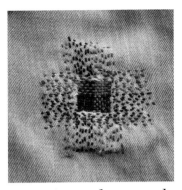

repair make mend
20

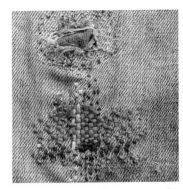

repair make mend
21

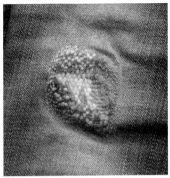

repair make mend
22

repair make mend
23

Damage: deterioration over time
Thread used: very fine wool yarn,
linen embroidery yarn, No. 25
embroidery thread, sashiko thread
How to make
Appliqué (see p26).

repair make mend
20–22, 25

Damage: ageing, damaged and torn.
Thread used: extra-fine woollen yarn,
extra-fine mohair, medium-fine woollen
yarn, sashiko thread
How to make
Darn the damaged part of the hole
and surrounding area with a seed and
square darn (see p20). Reverse appliqué
reinforced with seed stitch is used in 21
(see p27). Look at the balance and add
your favourite darn where you please.

The seed and square darn is
effective for denim where the fabric
has been damaged in large areas
and there are open holes.

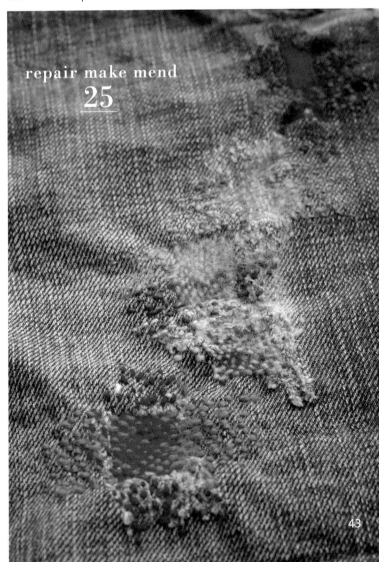

repair make mend
25

repair make mend
26

Damage: bleach and paint stains,
torn holes
Thread used: sashiko thread,
synthetic thread, hemp thread
How to make
Darn each stain and hole with
a square darn (see p16), seed
and square darn (see p20) or
tambourine darn (see p49).
Reinforce the cuffs and other items
with seed stitch (see p13).

There were various damaged parts, so I used a variety of techniques such as the square darn, seed and square darn and tambourine darn. When darning this garment I imaginined a starry night with a shooting star, and connected the darns with a seed stitch trail.

I added seed stitches around the sleeves and crest to complete the design. Even if you only darn one damaged part this will finish the item nicely.

Inspiration 1

Alternatives to the darning mushroom

I have a vague memory of my grandmother, who was born in 1905, darning socks using a light bulb as a darning mushroom. All sorts of everyday items can be used for darning.

In the photo above are some of the things I use most often. The first item on the left is a Venetian glass mushroom. It is smooth and light shines through it, which is extremely useful when you want to darn a thin blouse with fine detail.

The second item is a plastic toy capsule. When I did a darning workshop for students, we would use these capsules that had been discarded at gaming centres. They are excellent for storing needles and thread, although a little too curved.

The third item is an ostrich eggshell from a friend's ostrich ranch in South Africa. This kind of shell is suitable for darning big holes in the knees of denim trousers. The next item is a cowrie; in the Victorian era such shells were often used.

The decorative silver bowl – any bowl like this can be useful for darning large areas. I recommend a kokeshi doll with a flat head for general darning, and gourds because they are light and easy to hold, which is good for long periods of darning.

You can find countless substitutes, such as round or egg-shaped wooden blocks, figurines, car headlights, maracas, small watermelons... the list is endless.

Darning Technique 10　Chain darning

Embroidery techniques can be used for darning. The first technique is a chain stitch. Here it is stitched round and round, forming a spiral. By filling in the holes tightly you can reinforce worn fabric.

<< When to use >>

If the material is worn or damaged. Ideal for worn-out socks

Thread used:
Extra-fine mohair (light green)

1 | Place the worn-out area of the sock heel on the darning mushroom.

2 | Make a circular outline with a running stitch 5mm (¼in) outside the damaged area.

3 | Chain stitch anticlockwise around the outline.

4 | After you have gone all the way round, continue to chain stitch inside the first line.

5 | When the chain stitches reach the centre of the circle, push the thread through the centre to the back of the work and fasten off with a knot (see p18).

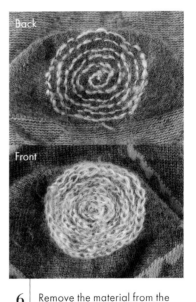

Back

Front

6 | Remove the material from the darning mushroom and you will get a finely woven darn. On the other side there will be a winding pattern. After sewing, apply gentle steam to set the threads.

Chain stitch

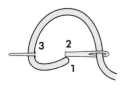

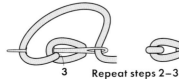

Repeat steps 2–3

Darning Technique 11　Honeycomb darn

If you make full use of blanket stitch, you can repair any damaged item. This method fills in the damaged part with stitches from the outside to the inside.

<< When to use >>

Worn or damaged fabric and a wide range of stains

Thread used:
Extra-fine mohair thread
(yellow, pink, orange)

1 Place the worn part of the heel on the darning mushroom and make an outline with running stitch 5mm (¼in) outside the damaged area.

2 Begin a row of blanket stitches along the ring. From outside the outline insert the needle towards the centre.

3 Pull the thread through.

4 Leave a slight gap, put the needle on the left side and thread it through, wrapping the yarn around the needle.

5 Repeat all around. After you have gone around once, put the needle through the first stitch and pull to close the ring.

6 Sew the second lap in the same way, starting from the inside line of the first lap towards the centre.

7 Continue, pointing the needle tip towards the centre when sewing, until you have completely covered the area.

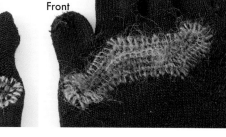

Back　　　　Front

8 Push the thread to the back and fasten off (see p18). Apply gentle steam to set the threads. The nice thing about blanket stitch is that the back is pretty as well.

Darning Technique 12 Tambourine darn

This is a quick and pretty way to cover small stains and marks. The tambourine-shaped motif is a variation of blanket stitch. Decorate an item with just one or many motifs.

Thread used: No. 25 embroidery thread (grey)

1 | Position the stained item centrally on the darning mushroom.

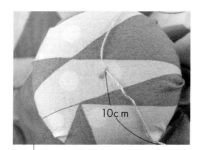

2 | As in step 2, insert the needle through the middle again, but exit slightly to the left. Pull the thread through.

3 | Put the needle in the middle of the stain and exit straight above, pulling the thread. Leave 10cm (4in) at the end.

4 | Repeat step 3 going anticlockwise.

5 | After you have gone around once, put the needle through the first stitch and pull to secure.

6 | Once you have pushed the thread to the back and tidied it (see p18), it is complete. It is also possible to make a larger circle by sewing a blanket stitch around the outside.

Blanket (buttonhole) stitch

Tambourine stitch

last stitch

Sew stitches close together to achieve a different effect.

Chapter 4 | Darning sweaters

A hole in a sweater can be tricky to fix, but if you can darn then it is easy!
Make the mend inconspicuous by using a similar type and shade of yarn,
or make it stand out by having fun with different materials and colours.

repair make mend
27

Damage: small holes of unknown cause
Thread used: extra-fine wool yarn,
extra-fine mohair yarn (two strings of
embroidered thread or sewing thread
are also acceptable)
How to make
Darn the hole with a square darn (see
p13). Variations of the triangle darn
(see p22) were added and tambourine
motifs scattered in places.

This is one of those thin sweaters that everyone has. After many years of wear small holes appear and became noticeable. After darning various shapes such as squares, triangles and rectangles and sewing some tambourine stitches it looks gorgeous.

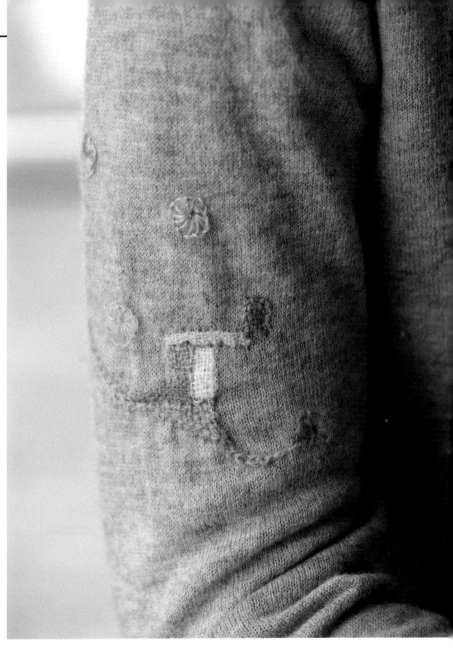

The holes in the cuffs were mended with a reversible square darn, which looks good when the cuffs are turned up.

51

Chapter 4

This navy colour is lovely and has been colourfully sewn with red, pink, yellow and blue wool.

repair make mend
28

Damage: damage of the whole sleeve over time
Thread used: extra-fine woollen yarn
How to make
Darn an L-shape variation of the square darn (see p22).

repair make mend
29

Damage: thread broken,
wear over time
Thread used: Shetland wool
How to make
Darn the severe damage
tightly with square darns (see
p16). Add a triangular darn
(see p22) next to the square.

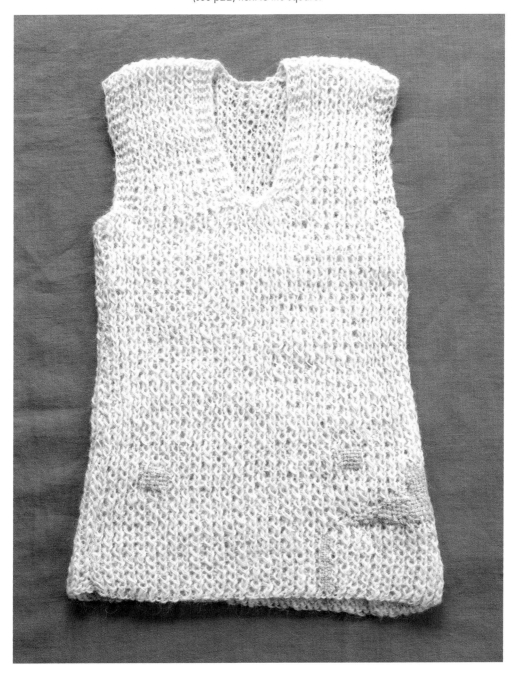

Make the whole design fit together by choosing wool or mohair yarns that are the same as or similar to the multicolour background. These darns are arranged in the image of a corsage.

Damage: small holes and stains from wear over time
Thread used: extra-fine woollen yarn, extra-fine mohair.
How to make
Make small square (see p16) and triangle (see p22) darns randomly over the stained area.

Imagining a refreshing early summer
stream, I darned long narrow triangles
each with a different colour tone, lustre
and type of cotton and linen threads also
known as summer thread.

repair make mend
31
Thread used: linen and cotton
sashiko thread
How to make
Darn triangles (see p22) in
a pattern around the
damaged area

Chapter 4

repair make mend
32

Damage: a tear between the material and the seam
Thread used: silk hand-sewing thread
How to make
Apply a thin cloth to the back to reinforce the fabric and then darn with seed and square darn (see p20). Use the seed stitch around the area to reinforce the seam and help the darn blend in.

repair make mend
33

Damage: Large stain.
Thread used:
Japanese paper thread, silk hand-sewing thread.
How to make
Use an accordion darn (see p25). First sew the warp with Japanese paper thread. Then sew the weft with silk hand-sewing thread using seed stitch.

Large stains on pale clothes that can't be bleached can be difficult to repair. Accordion darns are ideal for hiding marks over large and delicate areas.

repair make mend
34

Damage: thumbnail-sized
holes caused by moths.
Thread used: silk yarn
and wide velvet ribbon.
How to make
Reverse appliqué (see p27).

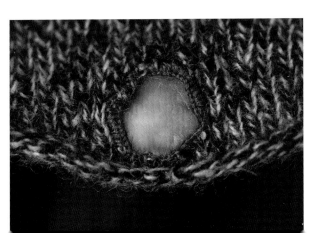

Use an iridescent glossy velvet
ribbon to match the texture of
the cashmere sweater. Stitch
around the hole with silk hand-
sewing thread to create a
brooch-like motif.

repair make mend
35

Damage: holes and tears
resulting from thread breakage
Thread used: extra-fine wool
How to make
Use a small square and seed
darn (see p20). Apply a
tambourine darn (see p49)
on the edge of the pocket.

This man's cardigan has extra-
fine wool yarn, so the same type of
yarn has been used to make it less
noticeable. Even if you decide to use
a bright colour the thread is thin so it
looks as if it was meant to be there.

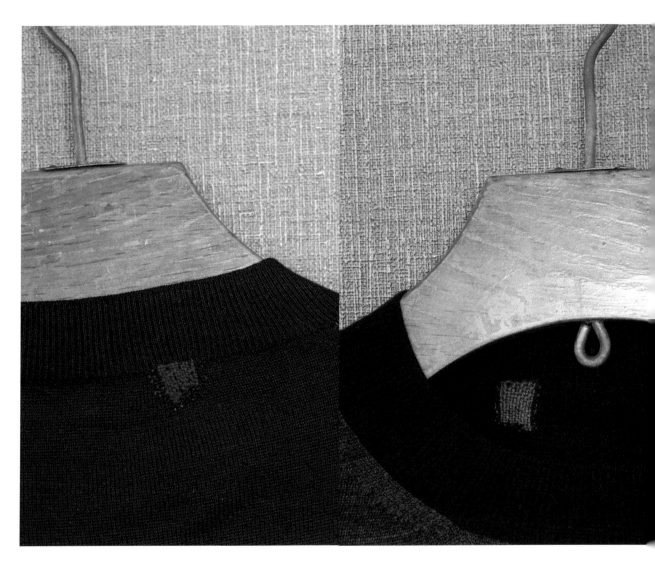

repair make mend
36

Damage: stitches on the back
along the seam have come undone
Thread used: extra-fine
woollen yarn
How to make
Apply an English darn
(see p24) on the front and
a square darn (see p19) on the
back along the seam.

| # Darning shirts

Shirts may have stains or become yellow with age. Choose the yarn thickness according to the thickness of the fabric and darn over the discolouration.

repair make mend
37

Damage: multiple coffee stains.
Thread used: medium-fine
woollen yarn with lamé
How to make
Draw an outline around the
stains using cups or glasses,
one small and one large to
form a gourd shape. Fill in
with honeycomb darn or leave
some of the centre free.

repair make mend
38

Damage: holes made by caught accessories and small stains.
Thread used: extra-fine lamé yarn

How to make

Use a square darn (see p16) over the hole and the stain. Then add more square darns to create an overall pattern.

In keeping with the gentle, floaty nature of the blouse, I delicately sprinkled 1cm (³⁄₈ in) square darns useing fine lamé thread.

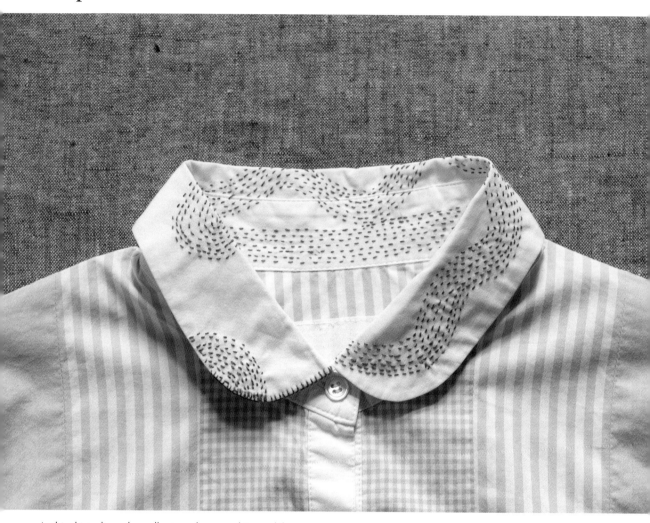

In this shirt where the collar is no longer white and the wear
is noticeable, I seed stitched a midsummer cloud design.
The corner of the collar is reinforced with blanket stitch.

repair make mend
39

Damage: yellowed by wear
over time
Thread used: embroidery
thread.
How to make
Darn the yellow areas on the
collar and cuffs with seed stitch
(see p13).

repair make mend
40

Damage: worn out from age
Thread used: hemp thread
How to make
Finely darn with seed stitch (see
p13) over the whole collar.

repair make mend
41

Damage: ageing and big holes
Thread used: hemp thread,
sashiko thread, synthetic thread
and extra-fine mohair
How to make
Reverse appliqué from the back.
You can sew it using either a
sewing machine or seed stitch
(see p26). In areas with severe
damage use a seed and square
darn (see p20). Darn the hem of
the slit with the seed and square
darn using sashiko thread.

Chapter 6 | Darning dresses

Mending a favourite dress will depend on the design, so be flexible.
Use a fine thread that blends into the fabric and a balanced design.

A stabbing motion with a single embroidery thread helps the stitches blend in with the fine woven fabric. A single tambourine darn is applied to a stain on the lower half of the dress.

repair make mend
42

Damage: wear and tear on the back of the dress
Thread used: silk sewing thread, polyester thread, embroidery thread
How to make
Fine English darn (see p24).

repair make mend
43

Damage: small moth-eaten holes
owing to long storage
Thread used: silk hand-sewing
thread and seed beads
How to make
Close the holes with square darn
(see p16) and add beads on top.
Stitch on the beads to make a
balanced pattern.

This dress is darned with hand-sewing
silk almost the same colour as the dress
and bright beads are added. Result: an
elegantly decorated chic black dress.

repair make mend
44

Damage:
Tears at the back of the dress
Thread used:
Polyester sewing thread
How to make
Appliqué from the top and sew
using seed stitch (see p26).

When delicate silk materials have holes
in them appliqué from either the top or
bottom and reinforce the repair with seed
stitch. I kept the balance by adding a
similar decoration to the front of the dress.

Inspiration 2

The links between craft and science

From left: Rik's shirt | Darned sport socks express the possibilities of contrast | A jumper from the shoddy factory of Annemor Sundbø, darned by Celia Pym

www.celiapym.com

In 2014, an interesting collaboration took place between textile artist Celia Pym, finalist of the Woman's Hour Craft Prize and Loewe Craft Prize 2017, and Dr Richard Wingate of the Developmental Neurology Department, King's College London. Celia graduated from the textile department at the Royal College of Art in the UK and is active in creating works that make use of knitting and darning. Richard is researching the 'psychological effects of anatomic training on medical students'. They discovered that darning and surgery have something in common: mending. So, they conducted an experiment in which Celia worked in a corner of the Dissecting Room to darn for three months. Every day Celia mended clothes brought in by medical students and teaching staff. From those who brought them in she would hear about their feelings about the clothes and the process of the damage,

gaining some understanding of their habits and lifestyle.

In the Dissecting Room the students practise on cadavers every day. Some students were disturbed by the unfamiliarity of the work, but in those moments they would casually sit next to Celia while she worked. Celia said, 'I go to the training room and I darn while talking to the students. No matter how well the repairs go the item will never be new again, but it will be usable, and it will bring affection. And it is the same with the body. While being in the same place I realised the importance of being there as we shared mending work like dissection (dissecting the damaged area), verification (looking closely at the degree of damage) and suturing (stitching).' Richard observed that Celia reduced the tension in the training room and, having similar healing intentions to the students, helped to still their minds.

Chapter 7 | Darning T-shirts

T-shirts that are washed and worn many times over, become tired. Partial darning around the collar and cuffs will refresh them, ready for more wear.

repair make mend
45

Thread used: raffia (aubergine, burnt orange, lilac and natural)
How to make
Cover the damaged parts using seed stitch (see p13) and chain stitch (see p47) following the design on the fabric.

Raffia is a natural material made from palm trees. Tear the material when using it to obtain the desired thickness. Instead of tidying the ends they have been left to provide fringes.

repair make mend

46

Damage: wear around the neck
owing to age.
Thread used: embroidery thread.
How to make
Use seed stitch (see p13) and
blanket stitch (see p49) around
the neck.

repair make mend

48

Damage: hole
Thread used: embroidery lamé
thread, beads
How to make
Use a square darn (see p16)
while weaving in beads. Seed
stitch (see p13) to adapt the
darning to the surroundings.

repair make mend

47

Damage: hole
Thread used: sashiko thread,
embroidery thread
How to make
Only use cotton yarn with a
cotton polo shirt. Darn with
seed and square (see p20).

repair make mend

49

Damage: wear around the
neck owing to age.
Thread used: sewing thread
How to make
Use a thread that is soft on the
skin and seed stitch (see p13).

Chapter 8 | Darning children's clothes

Children's clothes are quickly ripped or stained. They can be mended with darning and sometimes even improved with a favourite patch or topical appliqué.

repair make mend
50

Damage: small holes and stains
Thread used: sashiko thread,
sewing thread
How to make
Scatter darn variations such as
square (see p16), triangle and
L shape (see p22).

The long-sleeved T-shirt uses similar colours while the short-sleeved T-shirt uses blue thread. As there was damage all over, various shapes are scattered in a pattern. The knees of the trousers have a cute L-shaped and triangular accent.

repair make mend

51

Damage: small hole from thread breakage
Thread used: embroidery thread
How to make
Darn the hole with a square darn (see p16) and the damaged area with seed stitch (see p13).

repair make mend

52

Damage: hole in the knee
Thread used: synthetic hair yarn, medium hair yarn and extra-fine mohair yarn (nylon and acrylic blends are hardwearing)
How to make
Triangular darn (see p22).

repair make mend
53

Damage: discoloration around
the hems and collar
Thread used: sashiko thread
How to make
Darn with honeycomb darn (see
p48) along the outline of the
discoloured area.

I took advantage of the discoloured area by doing
a honeycomb darn with bright orange needlework
thread that matched the chest patch. It is quick, even
if used for a large area.

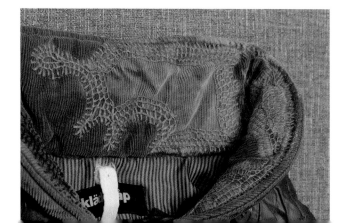

repair make mend
54

Damage: a worn hole in the knee
Thread used: sashiko thread and
hemp thread in black and white
How to make
Draw a circle around the hole
with a fabric marking pen. Stitch
along the marked area, sew the
horizontal thread to hide the
stitching and darn variation on
a square (see p22).

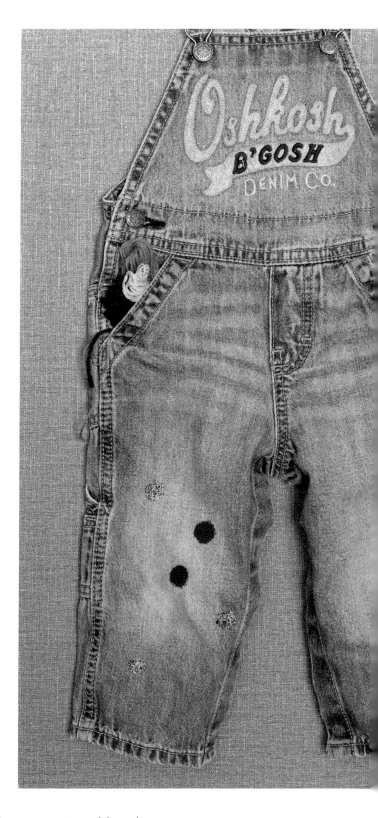

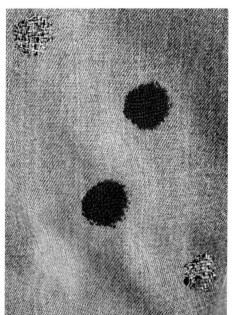

Choose your cotton sashiko and
hemp thread according to your
jeans fabric. The roundness of
polka dots goes well with denim.

Chapter 9 | Darning for interiors

Furnishing fabric can also be darned. Choose a strong yarn and you can mend tablecloths, blankets, cushion, and even sofas, neatly.

There was a lot of damage around the outer corner where the blanket had been folded for many years. Different thread thicknesses – thin, medium, thick – are scattered on the material because the material is thick. I chose a bright colour to stand out against the grey.

repair make mend
55

Damage: open seams and moth holes from ageing
Thread used: extra-fine thread, fine synthetic thread, thick synthetic thread and mohair yarn
How to make
Darn the damaged parts with seed and square stitch (see p20). Reinforce the edges with seed stitch (see p13).

Chapter 9

repair make mend
56

Damage: torn hole

Thread used: hemp yarn

How to make

Darn the hole with a seed and
square darn (see p20). Simple
hemp yarn was used to contrast
with the embroidery on the linen.

repair make mend
57

Damage: big holes and
scratches made by cats
Thread used: Shetland wool
How to make
Square and seed darn (see
p20). Use blanket stitch for the
border (see p49). Large holes
can be darned using a round
container or bowl.

Interior damage happens easily
in homes with pets, but with
square and seed stitch it is easy
to repair large holes. It will also
look beautiful on the back (see
picture below right).

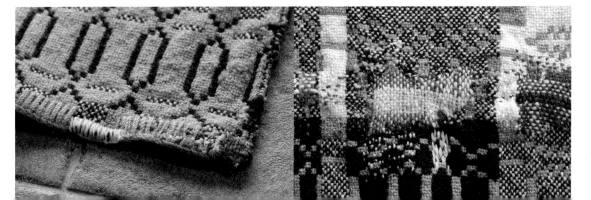

repair make mend
58

Damage: friction from ageing
and cat scratching
Thread used: mohair yarn
How to make
Appliqué fabric on the
damaged parts. Stitch from
above through all layers.

This embroidered fabric blends in
well with an antique velvet sofa
and covers the holes too. When
sewing on sofas use U-shaped
upholstery needles.

repair make mend
59

Damage: a wide range of
fabric damaged from ageing
Thread used: sashiko thread
How to make
From the centre of the circle
work a tambourine darn (see
p49). Then sew seed stitch
a few times around the circle.

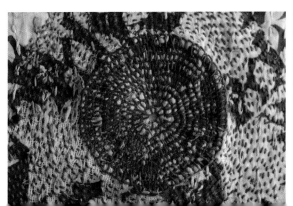

The tambourine darn is the best
to cover a large area. The fun
part of darning is that you can
sew as many darns as you like,
even when there's no hole or
stain to hide.

Chapter 10 | Darning accessories

When darning a thin shawl use fine thread. If darning a jute bag use thick Japanese paper thread. Choose your thread and stitch to match the material.

repair make mend

60

Damage: a tear that snagged
Thread used: Silk sewing
thread, lamé sewing thread
How to make
Finely sew an English darn (see
p24) so that the darn matches
the material.

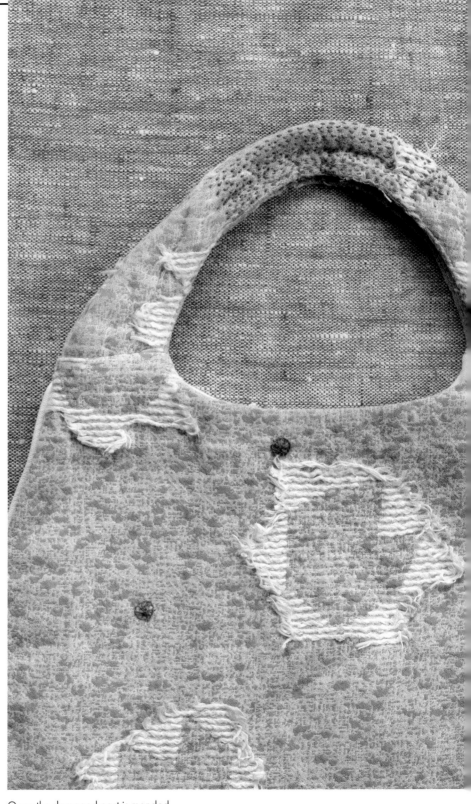

repair make mend
61

Damage: deterioration of the handle and small stains owing to regular use.
Thread used: hemp embroidery thread
How to make
Darn the handle with seed stitch (see p13). Tambourine darn (see p49) on the stains in the body of the bag.

Once the damaged part is mended, look at the whole and, if necessary, add stitches in other areas to balance the design.

repair make mend
63

Damage: ageing
Thread used: Japanese
paper yarn
How to make
Following the stitches of the
jute bag horizontally, darn a
heart shape.

repair make mend
62

Damage: discoloration
Thread used: Japanese paper
yarn
How to make
Use a spiral tambourine darn
(see p49). If you run out of
thread, change colour and
continue to sew.

When darning jute bags, choose a
compatible Japanese paper thread.
I used a charcoal grey so the heart motif
wouldn't be too pronounced.

Choosing a yarn for darning

Any thread you have at home can be used for darning. There are many types of thread and it is fun creating your own designs with them. Here are the main different types of threads I like to use and their characteristics.

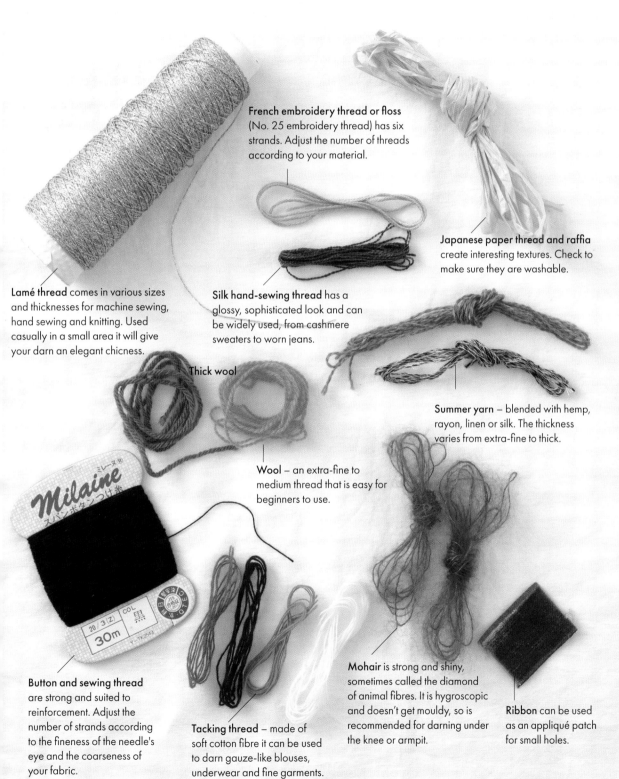

French embroidery thread or floss (No. 25 embroidery thread) has six strands. Adjust the number of threads according to your material.

Japanese paper thread and raffia create interesting textures. Check to make sure they are washable.

Lamé thread comes in various sizes and thicknesses for machine sewing, hand sewing and knitting. Used casually in a small area it will give your darn an elegant chicness.

Silk hand-sewing thread has a glossy, sophisticated look and can be widely used, from cashmere sweaters to worn jeans.

Thick wool

Summer yarn – blended with hemp, rayon, linen or silk. The thickness varies from extra-fine to thick.

Wool – an extra-fine to medium thread that is easy for beginners to use.

Button and sewing thread are strong and suited to reinforcement. Adjust the number of strands according to the fineness of the needle's eye and the coarseness of your fabric.

Tacking thread – made of soft cotton fibre it can be used to darn gauze-like blouses, underwear and fine garments.

Mohair is strong and shiny, sometimes called the diamond of animal fibres. It is hygroscopic and doesn't get mouldy, so is recommended for darning under the knee or armpit.

Ribbon can be used as an appliqué patch for small holes.

knitwear

You can use wool to mend wool knits, or, if you
dare, use cotton yarn to make the repair stand out.

Combining yarns and fabric ❶
Wool or cashmere sweater

To blend in the darns, the best yarn for wool is wool and for cashmere is cashmere, but dare to change the thread when darning. Try hemp yarn for fluffy sweaters and Shetland wool or brushed mohair yarn for soft and textured cashmere sweaters. If you want the darn to blend with the fabric, a thinner thread is better. The darn will be a feature if you choose a thicker, different-coloured thread.

Blanket stitch

English darn
Horizontal and vertical threads: Silk thread (olive green)

Square darn
Horizontal and vertical threads: ribbon thread (gold)

Accordion darn
Vertical threads: tweed thread (beige). Horizontal threads: silk sewing thread (orange)

Seed stitch
Cashmere yarn (mustard)

Tambourine darn
Polyester and nylon lamé (gold)

Seed stitch
Tacking thread (green)

Square darn
Vertical threads: medium fine thread (blue). Horizontal thread: medium fine thread (cyan)

Square darn
Horizontal and vertical threads: medium fine thread (lilac)

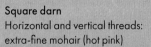

Square darn
Horizontal and vertical threads: extra-fine mohair (hot pink)

Square darn
Horizontal and vertical threads: cashmere (mustard). Repeat the horizontal thread twice and alternate it between two vertical threads

Square darn
Horizontal and vertical threads: cotton lace yarn (brick colour)

shirts

Choose earthy colours for natural-looking shirts. Hemp or other natural yarns, sewn loosely, will be in keeping.

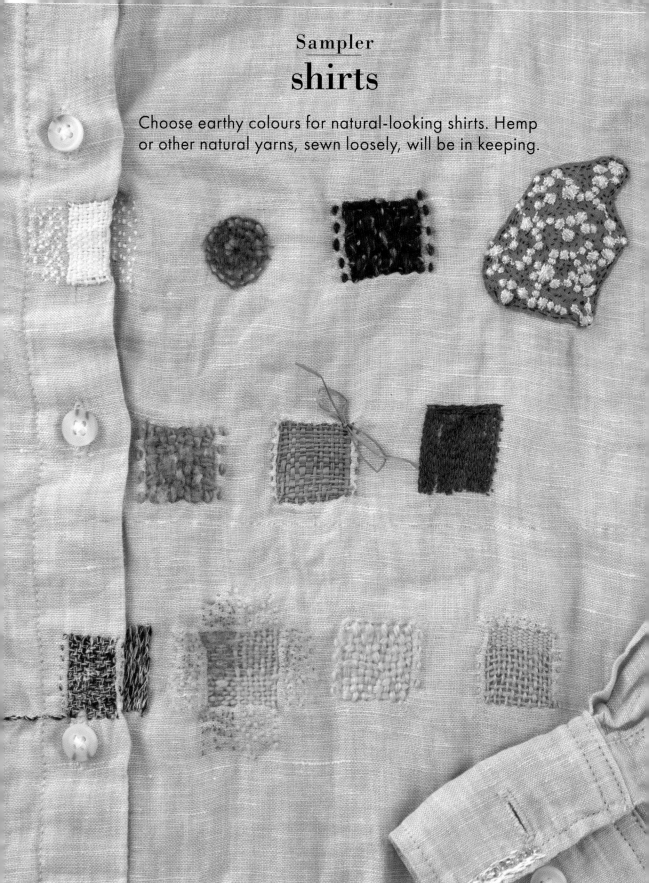

Combining yarns and fabric ❷
Woven fabrics such as shirts and chinos

When a fabric is not elastic it can be difficult to darn, plus it may be closely woven, so the needle might not enter easily. Try using a thread that is smooth, embroidery or sewing thread for example: embroidery thread can be adjusted to one, two or three strands depending on the thickness of the fabric and the size of the stitches. Tacking thread is soft, so it is perfect for gauze or soft materials – for thick shirts and chinos, durable sashiko thread is the best choice.

Seed and square
Horizontal and vertical threads: No. 25 embroidery thread (white)

Tambourine darn
Extra fine mohair (grey)

Square darn
Horizontal and vertical threads: tweed yarn (black)

Top appliqué and seed stitch
Metallic sewing threads (black)

Square darn
Horizontal and vertical threads: very thick tweed yarn (natural)

Square darn
Horizontal and vertical threads: raffia thread (lilac)

Chain stitch
Horizontal and vertical threads: cotton thread (peacock green)

Seed stitch (reverse)
Summer yarn (black and white)

Square darn
Horizontal and vertical threads: summer yarn (black and white)

Seed and square
Vertical threads: mohair yarn (blue grey), cashmere yarn (light blue). Horizontal threads: mohair silk yarn (lilac), cashmere yarn (light blue)

Square darn
Vertical and horizontal threads medium-fine cotton

Square darn
Vertical and horizontal threads: medium fine hemp

Seed stitch
Embroidery thread (white), beads (silver)

polo shirts

Choose colourful threads for a classic polo
shirt for style. Any material is okay for
polo shirts: wool, cotton, linen etc.

Combining yarns and fabric ❸
Polo shirts, T-shirts, sweatshirts

The stretchy cotton material of these garments is compatible with natural threads such as cotton and hemp. You can use embroidery thread, cotton thread, tacking thread and sashiko thread. If you would like a more interesting darn, raffia and Japanese paper thread stand out well. Of course, you can just use woollen yarn; it is fun to make changes to the wool like shrinking it in the wash after darning. However, it is recommended that you use a tough hygroscopic thread such as extra-fine mohair yarn.

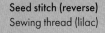

Seed stitch (reverse)
Sewing thread (lilac)

Square darn
Horizontal and vertical threads: No. 25 embroidery thread, two threads (orange), extra-fine mohair thread (yellow)

Triangular darn
Horizontal and vertical threads: summer-weight yarn (green)

Accordion darn
Vertical thread: Japanese paper thread (Navy). Horizontal thread: No. 25 embroidery thread (hot pink)

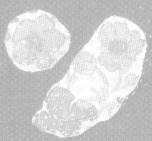

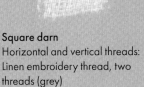

L-shaped darn
Horizontal and vertical threads: cotton thread (pink)

Top appliqué and seed stitch
Sewing thread (light pink, silver)

Square darn
Horizontal and vertical threads: Linen embroidery thread, two threads (grey)

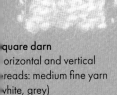

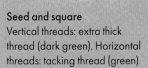

Square darn
Horizontal and vertical threads: medium fine yarn (white, grey)

Square darn
Horizontal and vertical threads: extra-fine woollen thread, three threads (orange)

Square darn
Horizontal and vertical thread: summer yarn (cyan)

Seed and square
Vertical threads: extra thick thread (dark green). Horizontal threads: tacking thread (green)

denim

Darning goes well with denim, so have fun using your
favourite threads, even if you appliqué the hole first.

Denim

Denim is perfect for any material or colour. Worn denim is surprisingly soft and easy to darn. Not only is it nice to darn with cotton and linen, but animal-based threads such as wool, mohair and cashmere, shiny threads such as rayon and silk, and lamé thread and ribbon are also wonderful to darn with. After denim has been repaired, the surrounding areas may suddenly weaken. If this happens you have another chance to darn. Repair the area in such a way that the second darn overlaps the first one a little.

Accordion darn
Vertical threads: medium fine thread (blue), extra-fine thread (yellow).
Horizontal threads: sewing thread (pink)

Accordion darn
Vertical threads: Japanese paper thread (unbleached).
Horizontal threads: silk thread (orange)

Square darn
Horizontal and vertical threads: extra-fine mohair (space dyed)

Top appliqué and seed stitch
Metallic sewing threads (silver), beads (grey)

Chain stitch
Extra-fine mohair thread (light beige)

Honeycomb darning
No. 25 embroidery thread, two threads (yellow green)

Seed and square
Horizontal and vertical threads: sashiko thread (space dyed)

Square darn
Horizontal and vertical threads: medium fine thread (light blue)

Reverse appliqué and seed stitch
Metallic sewing thread (gold)

Square darn
Horizontal and vertical threads: wool and cotton yarn (pink)

Square darn
Horizontal and vertical threads: summer-weight yarn (light grey)

Square darn
Vertical threads: raffia thread (red). Horizontal threads: raffia (lilac).

Seed stitch
No. 25 embroidery thread, two threads (yellow green)

Collection of patterns: denim and socks

Jeans and socks get damaged everywhere. Here,
to inspire you in your darning, I have chosen details
that could not be fully introduced in the main part.

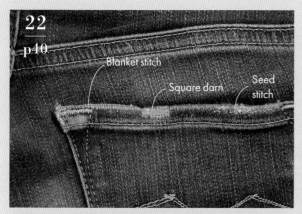

22
p40

Blanket stitch

Square darn

Seed
stitch

25
p41

Blanket stitch

21
p40

Square
darns

Seed stitch

Chain stitch

Square darn

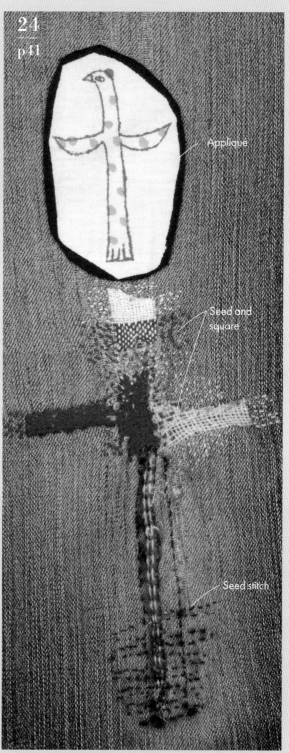

24
p41

Appliqué

Seed and
square

Seed stitch

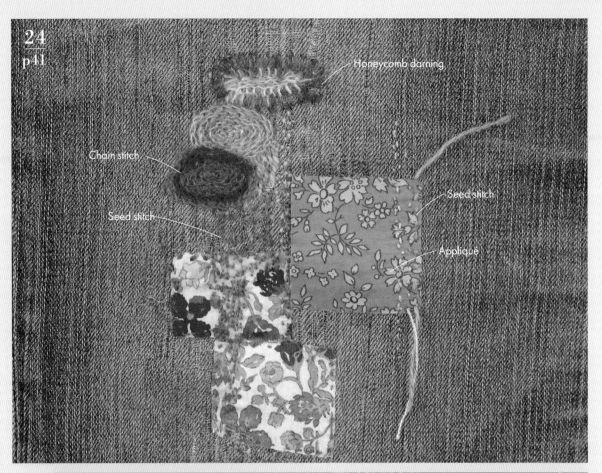

24 p41

Honeycomb darning

Chain stitch

Seed stitch

Seed stitch

Appliqué

25 p41

Seed and square

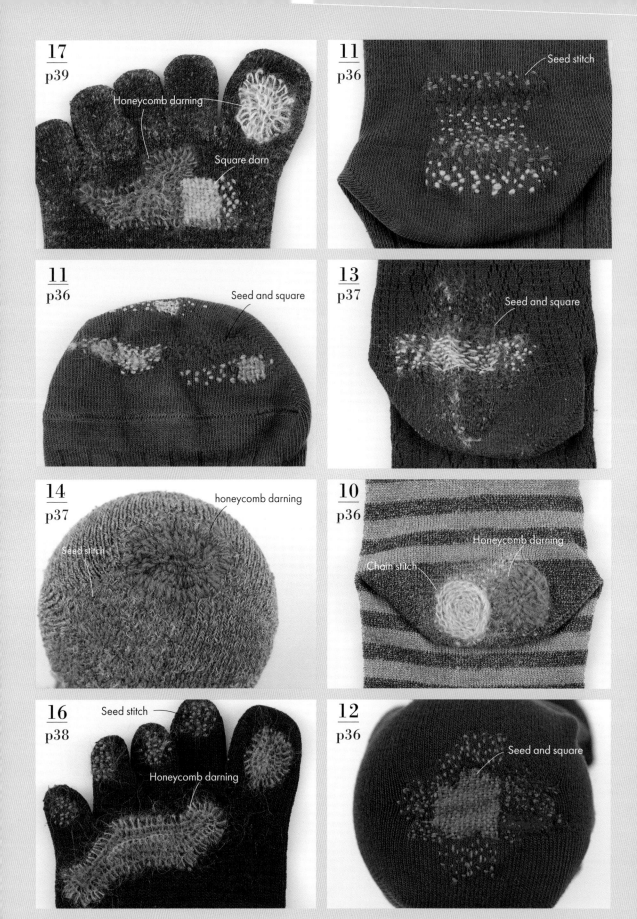

17 p39 — Honeycomb darning / Square darn

11 p36 — Seed stitch

11 p36 — Seed and square

13 p37 — Seed and square

14 p37 — honeycomb darning / Seed stitch

10 p36 — Chain stitch / Honeycomb darning

16 p38 — Seed stitch / Honeycomb darning

12 p36 — Seed and square

Afterword

I have been astonishingly blessed with the opportunity to teach darning to so many people over the past five years, despite being told that no one would want to keep wearing mended socks when you can buy three pairs for 1000 yen or £5. We created a workshop for those who cherished hope that they could do something for the clothes they had tried to throw away but couldn't, even though the damage was severe.

You meet people with these kinds of stories, people who want to take over the task from their mothers, and those who want to use neglected sewing materials in darning. From these different encounters I was able to develop my own method of using and choosing yarns and stitches.

As you can see from the 63 examples in this book, because of the way the clothes are damaged, the threads, stitches, colours and shapes have to be used creatively. Darning is the method to prolong the life of clothes. If you think, 'I want to use it a little longer, no, much longer', then it is up to you to determine the item's lifespan. I hope darning may become a life-long friend for even more people.

Once again, I would like to thank former editor-in-chief of Keitodama, Kumiko Aoki, who supported my darning activities from early on; lifestyle stylist, living room renovator and DIY leader Kanae Ishii; the employees of Mina Perhonen who provided me with lots of damaged clothes; all of Nippon Vogue's employees; and everybody from Keito, Tomomi Akaiwa, Makiko Tezuka, Ken, Kubo-chan, Hiromi and the 'repair make mend' production team.

Hikaru Noguchi

Knit designer Hikaru Noguchi presides over the eponymous knit brand Hikaru Noguchi. After graduating from Musashino Art University, Tokyo, she studied textile design at Middlesex University in the United Kingdom. Based in Tokyo, she has been publishing design collections for twenty-five years. She has expanded her activities all over the world, including textile design, consulting and writing. During the last few years, as an instigator of darning, she has held classes and workshops all over the world. She also creates her own original darning mushrooms and patterns.

Website: www.hikarunoguchi.com
Workshops and product information: www.darning.net
Instagram: @hikaru_noguchi_design

These are our recommended suppliers and shops. In addition, you may wish to support your local haberdashery.

Habu
habutextiles.com habu@habutextiles.com
Knit with Attitude
127 Stoke Newington High Street, London N16 0PH
+44 (0)20 7998 3282 sales@knitwithattitude.com
knitwithattitude.com
Loop
15 Camden Passage, Islington, London N1 8EA
+44 (0)20 7288 1160 shop@loopknitting.com
loopknittingshop.com
MacCulloch and Wallis
25–26 Poland Street, London W1F 8QN
+44 (0)20 7629 0311 mailorder@macculloch.com
macculloch-wallis.co.uk
Purl Soho
459 Broome Street, New York, New York 10013
+1 212(800) 597 PURL customerservice@purlsoho.com
Raystitch
66–68 Essex Road, London N1 8LR
+44 (0)20 7704 1060 info@raystitch.co.uk
raystitch.co.uk

Wild and Woolly
116 Lower Clapton Road, London E5 0QR
+44 (0)20 8985 5231
info@wildandwoollyshop.co.uk
wildandwoollyshop.co.uk
Morris & Sons
50 York Street
Sydney NSW 2000
+61 (0)2 9299 8588
sydneystore@morrisandsons.com.au
morrisandsons.com.au
JM Embroideries & Collectibles
122 Commercial Road, Morwell, Vic. 3840
+61 (0)417670160
jmembroideriesmorwell@gmail.com
embroideries.com.au
L'uccello
The Nicholas Building, 37 Swanston Street,
Melbourne 3000
+61 (0)3 9639 0088 info@luccello.com.au
luccello.com.au

UK edition: Published in English by Hawthorn Press Ltd 2019
Translation: Camille White | Editor: Katy Bevan | © Hikaru Noguchi 2019
Printed by Short Run Press Ltd Exeter 2019. Reprinted 2021, 2023
British Library Cataloguing in Publication Data applied for
ISBN 978-1-912480-15-9
Orders from www.hawthornpress.com or trade at www.booksource.net

Hawthorn Press

NOGUCHI HIKARU NO DARNING DE REPAIR MAKE (NV70500)
© Hikaru Noguchi / NIHON VOGUE-SHA 2018 All rights reserved.
English translation rights arranged with NIHON VOGUE Corp. through Japan UNI Agency, Inc., Tokyo.
Photography: Wakana Baba, Noriaki Moryia | Stylist: Kanae Ishi | Model: Eriko Seki
Book design: Fumie Terayama | Editorial: Natsuko Sugawara